Laurence Main

**Kittiwake Press in association with
John Bartholomew & Son Ltd**

Also in this series:
Guide to the Western Islands of Scotland
Guide to the Dyfi Valley Way

Published by
The Kittiwake Press in association with
John Bartholomew & Son Ltd,
Duncan Street, Edinburgh EH9 1TA.

Great care has been taken to be accurate. The publishers
cannot, however, accept responsibility for any errors which
may appear, or their consequences.

This route is believed to follow well established rights of
way, or accepted diversions. Please always KEEP TO THE PATH.
Remember that it is a privilege to cross private land, so do
not spoil things for those who follow you.

Editor: David Perrott

Photographs: Laurence Main

Drawings: Morag Perrott

Typesetting: Perrott Cartographics, Darowen, Machynlleth
and Litho Link Limited, Welshpool

Litho origination: Litho Link Limited, Welshpool

Printing and binding: Richard Clay, Bungay, Suffolk

Front cover: The River Thames at Abingdon *top left*;
Dorchester Abbey *top right*; Approaching Castle
Hill, Wittenham Clumps *bottom*.

ISBN 0 7028 0915 2

1/3.0/5-89

Introduction

The countryside around Oxford offers variety and scenic beauty, whilst being easy to walk. Although generally low-lying, there are many fine viewpoints, such as over the remote area of Otmoor from Beckley, across the Thames Valley from Wittenham Clumps or towards the Downs from Jarn Mound. The towing paths of the River Thames and of the Oxford Canal bring a special peace and tranquillity, and provide a glimpse of water wildlife. The sense of history is great, with Sir Winston Churchill's birthplace at Blenheim Palace and grave at Bladon. Edward the Confessor was baptised at Islip, while Dorchester Abbey marks the site of the first cathedral in Wessex.

There is no better way of exploring this area than on foot. This guide consists of a strip map at a scale of 4 inches to 1 mile, marking in such details as stiles, gates and signposts, while a walk profile gives an impression of the ups and downs. Information about public transport, accommodation, shops and cafés is included. There are notes on interesting places to visit and plenty of photographs and drawings.

Read the strip map from the bottom to the top of each page (when walking clockwise) so that the map faces the direction in which you walk. As this means that north cannot always be at the top of the page, the direction of north is shown on each page. The sheet number of the relevant Ordnance Survey Pathfinder map is also given, so that the strip map can be related to the surrounding countryside. The whole of this route is contained on the Ordnance Survey Landranger map of Oxford (sheet 164).

The Oxfordshire Trek is a long distance walk which can be very easily divided into short sections, since it encircles Oxford, from where bus and train routes radiate like the spokes of a wheel. Although there is accommodation along the route, a central base in Oxford, which has a youth hostel and campsites, may be preferred.

Order of content

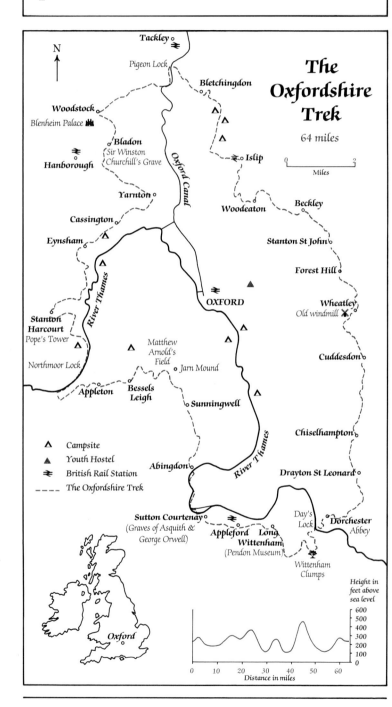

The Oxfordshire Trek

64 miles

Tackley

Pigeon Lock

Bletchingdon

Woodstock

Blenheim Palace

Bladon
Sir Winston Churchill's Grave

Hanborough

Islip

Yarnton

Woodeaton

Beckley

Cassington

Stanton St John

Eynsham

River Thames

Oxford Canal

Forest Hill

OXFORD

Wheatley
Old windmill

Stanton Harcourt
Pope's Tower

Northmoor Lock

Matthew Arnold's Field

Jarn Mound

Cuddesdon

Appleton

Bessels Leigh

Sunningwell

Chiselhampton

Campsite

Youth Hostel

British Rail Station

The Oxfordshire Trek

Abingdon

River Thames

Drayton St Leonard

Sutton Courtenay
(Graves of Asquith & George Orwell)

Appleford

Long Wittenham
(Pendon Museum)

Day's Lock

Dorchester
Abbey

Wittenham Clumps

Oxford

Height in feet above sea level

600
500
400
300
200
100
0

0   10   20   30   40   50   60
Distance in miles

Miles
0   2

Mileage and facilities

Place	Page	Mile	Train	Bus	Campsite	B&B	Shop	Café or pub	Post Office	Bank	Launderette	Early closing day
Bladon	6&59	60&64	H	R				✓	✓	✓		
Woodstock	8	2		✓		✓	✓	✓	✓	✓	✓	W
Bletchingdon	14	8	T	✓	✓	✓	✓	✓	✓	✓		W
Islip	16	11	✓	G	✓	✓	✓	✓	✓	✓		S
Stanton St John	23	18		✓				✓	✓			
Forest Hill	25	19		✓			✓		✓			
Wheatley	26	21		✓				✓	✓	✓		
Cuddesdon	28	23				✓		✓	✓	✓		W S
Chislehampton	29	26				✓			✓			
Dorchester	32	30		✓		✓		✓	✓	✓		Tu
L. Wittenham	36	35						✓	✓	✓		W S
Appleford	38	37	✓									
Sut. Courtenay	41	39						✓	✓	✓		
Abingdon	42	41		✓		✓	✓	✓	✓	✓	✓	✓	Th
Boars Hill	46	44		✓		✓			✓			
Bessels Leigh	48	47			✓				✓			
Appleton	49	48		✓				✓	✓	✓		Tu
Stn. Harcourt	52	55				✓	✓		✓			
Eynsham	55	58		✓	✓	✓	✓	✓	✓	✓	✓	W
Yarnton	58	61		✓					✓			

B&B	Bed & Breakfast in farmhouse, guesthouse or hotel
H	Hanborough station, one mile west of Bladon on A4095
T	Tackley station, one mile north of Pigeon Lock by bridlepath
R	Bus stop at roundabout where A4095 meets A34 (one mile east)
G	Bus stop at Gosford. Turn south along the A43 for one mile from the Islip turn. South Midland buses 123 – 127 to Oxford
Tu	Tuesdays
W	Wednesdays
Th	Thursdays
S	Saturdays

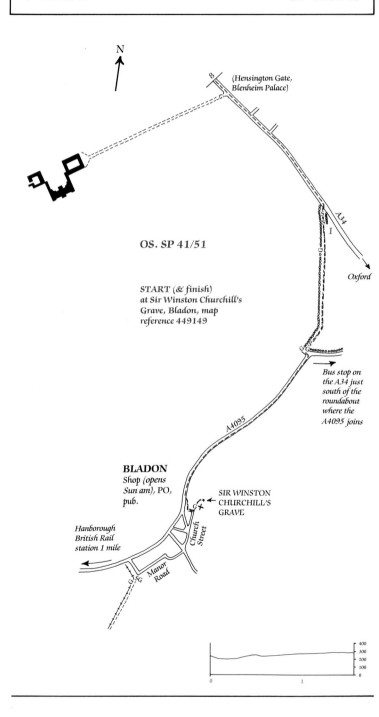

N

(Hensington Gate,
Blenheim Palace)

A34

1

Oxford

OS. SP 41/51

START (& finish)
at Sir Winston Churchill's
Grave, Bladon, map
reference 449149

*Bus stop on
the A34 just
south of the
roundabout
where the
A4095 joins*

A4095

BLADON
*Shop (opens
Sun am), PO,
pub.*

SIR WINSTON
CHURCHILL'S
GRAVE

*Hanborough
British Rail
station 1 mile*

Church Street

Manor Road

400
300
200
100
0

0   1

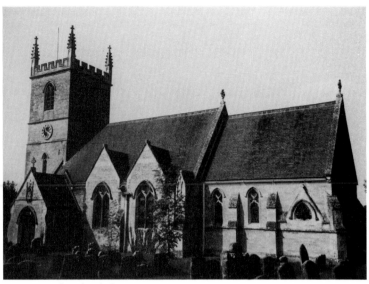

St Martin's church, Bladon.

BLADON   (mile 0 & 64)

The Oxfordshire Trek starts and finishes at St Martin's church, Bladon. This little churchyard was where Sir Winston Churchill chose to be buried. Described in the last years of his public service as 'the greatest living Englishman', Sir Winston Churchill died on 24th January, 1965, exactly 70 years to the day after his father, Lord Randolph Churchill, who was the second son of the seventh Duke of Marlborough and the first member of the family to be buried at Bladon. Sir Winston Churchill's funeral was held in St Paul's Cathedral, London, but his body was interred here on 30th January, 1965. His wife, Clementine, died on 12th December, 1977, and her ashes were interred in the same grave as her husband on 16th December. Bladon is now visited by very many American tourists (Sir Winston's mother was American) but it remains unspoilt. It is named after the nearby river (now called the Evenlode, but once called the Bladene) and the settlement dates back at least to the Romans. The Domesday Book recorded the place as Blade in 1086. Henry II and Thomas à Becket came here, while the Black Prince was brought up in the area. The local limestone was famous and was used to build Merton College and the Sheldonian Theatre in Oxford. Glove making was a local cottage industry, while many villagers were employed in the construction of Blenheim Palace in the early 18th century. Later, they served on the estate. Nowadays, Bladon can be described as a commuter village.

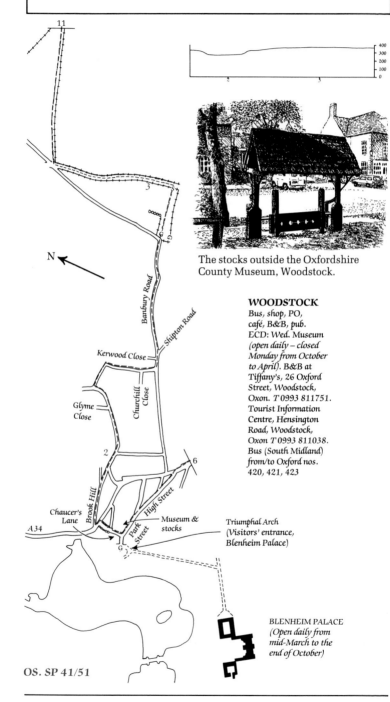

The stocks outside the Oxfordshire
County Museum, Woodstock.

WOODSTOCK
*Bus, shop, PO,
café, B&B, pub.
ECD: Wed. Museum
(open daily – closed
Monday from October
to April). B&B at
Tiffany's, 26 Oxford
Street, Woodstock,
Oxon. T 0993 811751.
Tourist Information
Centre, Hensington
Road, Woodstock,
Oxon T 0993 811038.
Bus (South Midland)
from/to Oxford nos.
420, 421, 423*

N

11

3

Banbury Road

Shipton Road

Kerwood Close

Churchill Close

Glyme Close

2

6

Chaucer's Lane

Brook Hill

A34

Park Street

High Street

G

Museum & stocks

*Triumphal Arch
(Visitors' entrance,
Blenheim Palace)*

*BLENHEIM PALACE
(Open daily from
mid-March to the
end of October)*

OS. SP 41/51

Turn down Chaucer's Lane, Woodstock.

Go down these steps at the end of Chaucer's Lane, Woodstock.

WOODSTOCK (mile 2)

Woodstock has had royal associations since Saxon times. Kings hunted from the royal manor here, which was walled in the 12th century to contain the deer. Henry II's mistress, Fair Roz, Rosamund Clifford, lived nearby and gave her name to the well on the north bank of Blenheim Lake. She was found dead in her bower despite being protected from the jealous Queen Eleanor by a labyrinth whose path was known only by the king.

On 17th February, 1705, Queen Anne conferred the 'Honour and manor of Woodstock' on John Churchill, 1st Duke of Marlborough, in recognition and gratitude for his services to the country during the war against the French. This included 'that demolished messuage, courthouse or toft . . . called Woodstock Manor House, and all that piece or parcel of ground commonly called Woodstock Park . . . containing in the whole by estimation 1,793 acres and two roods'. A new, grander, palace was to arise, to be called Blenheim, after the site of the battle at Blindheim in Bavaria where six months earlier Marlborough, with Eugene, had defeated the French army. John Vanbrugh was the chosen architect and Capability Brown transformed the huge park into a 'naturalistic' landscape. The grand approach from Woodstock through the Triumphal Arch is outstanding. 'As we passed through the entrance archway and the lovely scenery burst upon me', wrote Lady Randolph Churchill on her first visit to Blenheim, Randolph said with pardonable pride, 'This is the finest view in England. Looking at the lake, the bridge, the miles of magnificent park studded with old oaks . . . and the huge and stately palace, I confess I felt awed. But my American pride forbade the admission'.

'At Blenheim', Sir Winston Churchill was known to declare, 'I took two very important decisions; to be born and to marry. I am happily content with the decisions I took on both occasions'.

There is more to Woodstock than Blenheim Palace. The Oxfordshire Trek passes the Oxfordshire County Museum, outside which stand the stocks. In 'The Pattern of the Past' (1969), Guy Underwood noted that stocks are located where three water lines emerge from a blind spring to make an angle of less than 45°, with the stocks on the central line. This produced two U symbols facing away from the spring and towards the prisoner, forming the symbol of protection and mercy by the Mother Goddess. It was believed that this pattern of water lines would have produced a small and gradual effect on the nervous system which would have smitten the culprit with a sense of dejection and gloom.

The Triumphal Arch (the visitors' entrance), Blenheim Palace.

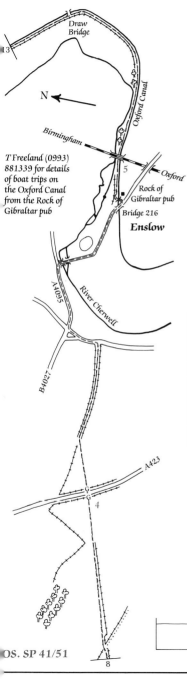

THE OXFORD CANAL   (mile 5-6)

The Oxford Canal was completed in 1790 to improve transport between the Midlands and the Thames Valley. It made coal much cheaper to buy in Oxford and gave water access to London. The opening of the Grand Junction Canal (now the Grand Union) in 1800 gave a more direct route to the capital from the Midlands, and succeeded in drawing traffic away from the older canal. The Oxford Canal maintained its viability however, by charging outrageously high tolls for a short section it shared with the Grand Junction between Braunston and Napton. Today the Oxford Canal is one of the most popular pleasure cruising routes on the canal network (see Ordnance Survey Guide to the Waterways, no 1, South, ed. David Perrott).

From the gate after crossing the A423, go ahead to the old tree-lined green lane. This ploughed footpath should be reinstated. Keep to the line of the right of way.

T Freeland (0993) 881339 for details of boat trips on the Oxford Canal from the Rock of Gibraltar pub

Looking west from the bridge across the River Cherwell, near Enslow.

Pleasure craft on the Oxford Canal, Enslow.

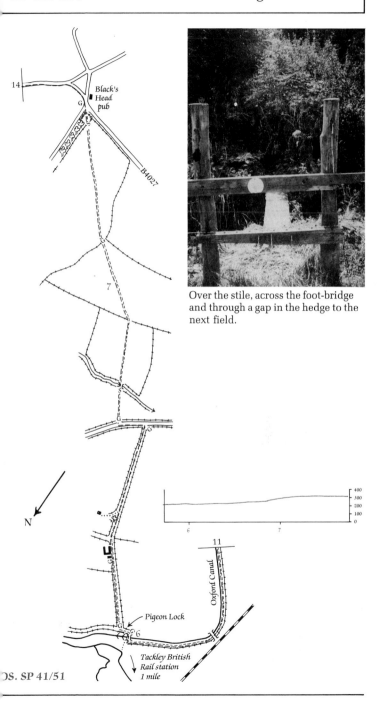

Over the stile, across the foot-bridge
and through a gap in the hedge to the
next field.

14

Black's
Head
pub

B4027

N

400
300
200
100
0

6   7

11

Oxford Canal

Pigeon Lock

6

Tackley British
Rail station
1 mile

BLETCHINGDON **(mile 8)**

Bletchingdon Park was once the seat
of Lord Valentia. It is now a School
of English Studies, catering mainly
for Arabs. A medallion portrait on
the wall of a house marks where
Cromwell slept in the Islip Road
during the Civil War.

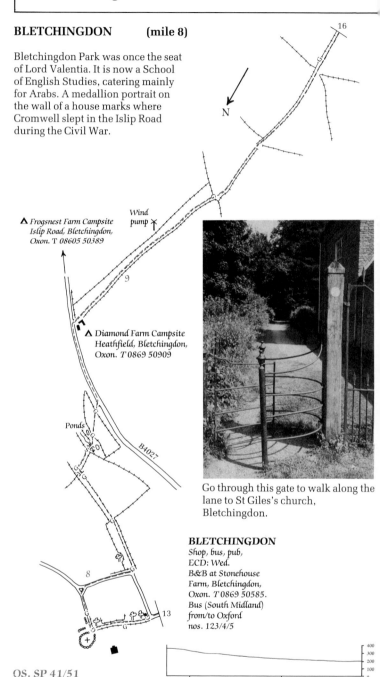

16

N

Wind
pump

▲ *Frogsnest Farm Campsite*
Islip Road, Bletchingdon,
Oxon. T 08605 50389

9

▲ *Diamond Farm Campsite*
Heathfield, Bletchingdon,
Oxon. T 0869 50909

Ponds

B4027

8

13

Go through this gate to walk along the
lane to St Giles's church,
Bletchingdon.

BLETCHINGDON
Shop, bus, pub,
ECD: Wed.
B&B at Stonehouse
Farm, Bletchingdon,
Oxon. T 0869 50585.
Bus (South Midland)
from/to Oxford
nos. 123/4/5

OS. SP 41/51

400
300
200
100
0

8   9

The path south-east of Bletchingdon.

Looking BACK at a fine example of a headland path south of Bletchingdon.
Headland paths should never be ploughed.

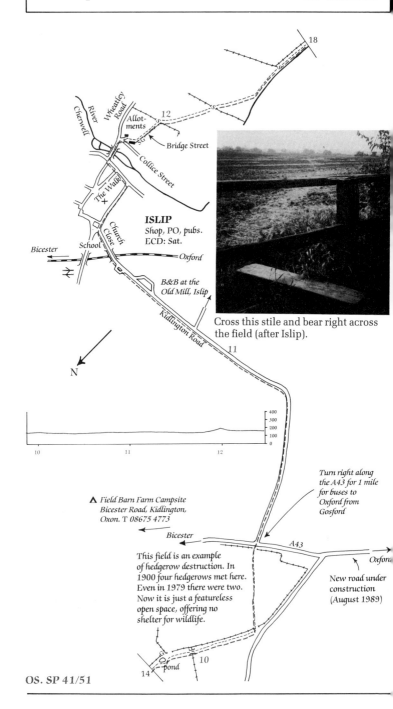

18

Wheatley Road

River Cherwell

Allotments

12

SG

Bridge Street

Collice Street

The Walks

ISLIP
Shop, PO, pubs.
ECD: Sat.

Church Close

School

Bicester ←

→ *Oxford*

B&B at the
Old Mill, Islip

Kidlington Road

11

Cross this stile and bear right across
the field (after Islip).

N

400
300
200
100
0

10   11   12

*Turn right along
the A43 for 1 mile
for buses to
Oxford from
Gosford*

⛺ *Field Barn Farm Campsite
Bicester Road, Kidlington,
Oxon. T 08675 4773*

Bicester ←

A43

→ *Oxford*

This field is an example
of hedgerow destruction. In
1900 four hedgerows met here.
Even in 1979 there were two.
Now it is just a featureless
open space, offering no
shelter for wildlife.

*New road under
construction
(August 1989)*

14   pond   10

ISLIP

(mile 11)

Islip is a beautiful village near the confluence of the rivers Ray and Cherwell. Its most impressive building is St Nicholas's Church, which is where Edward the Confessor was baptised. This Saxon king was born at Islip in 1004 and he gave the manor of Islip to Westminster Abbey when he built it. John of Islip became Prior of Westminster in 1500, while Simon of Islip became Archbishop of Canterbury in 1348. The bridge over the River Ray to the south of the village was an important outpost in the Royalist defence of their Oxford headquarters. The Royalists were defeated here by Cromwell in 1645. Later, as a staging post on the old London to Worcester road, Islip had 21 inns, but only two remain. The old village school was endowed by the rector, Dr South, in 1710. Dean Buckland, the famous geologist, is buried in the churchyard. Islip used to have a station on the Oxford to Bicester railway line. This line was reopened on an experimental basis in 1988.

The tower of St Nicholas's church, Islip.

WOODEATON   (mile 14)   OS. SP 41/51

Woodeaton was a prime example of a decayed village until some new houses were built recently. Don't rush through, however, as the church is one of the most interesting along this route. It is particularly relevant to long distance walkers as it has a 14th century wall painting of St Christopher carrying the Christ child facing the door (so that passers-by could see it), with a Norman-French inscription which means: 'Look upon this image and verily on this day you shall not die an evil death'. On the hottest day of the year, your author was revived by a kind lady in the house next to the church refilling his water bottle with marvellously pure, fresh water just after seeing this St Christopher. The church excels itself with a minstrel's gallery, a manorial pew, a rood beam with a doom inscription and a 13th century tower unusually built inside the church.

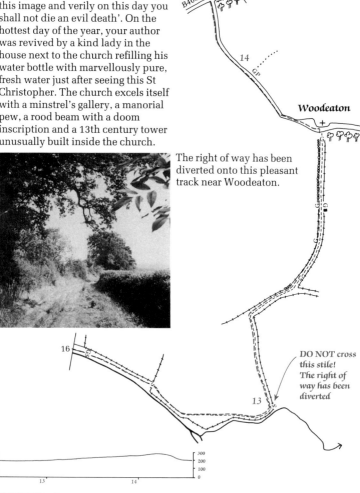

The right of way has been diverted onto this pleasant track near Woodeaton.

DO NOT cross this stile! The right of way has been diverted

Church of the Holy Rood, Woodeaton.

Go through this gateway along the track to Lower Woods Farm.

Walk across this field to the far corner.

23

OS. SP 41/51

BECKLEY   (mile 16)

N ←

Beckley
Pub.

+   16

Noke
Wood

This obstruction
has been reported.
Hopefully a gate
or stile will be
erected in this
fence soon.

Wire gate

15

Lower
Woods
Farm

View of
TV mast

18

Beckley is a delightful stone village
on a ridge overlooking Otmoor. This
manor was given to Robert D'Oily by
William the Conqueror and there are
still local property owners called
Deeley. The church of the Blessed
Virgin Mary includes 13th century
wall paintings of the Virgin and
child. The font dates from the 12th
century, while the pulpit is Jacobean
(1603-25). The church was originally
built to face the sunrise on 22nd
August, the Octave day of the Feast
of the Assumption. It was rebuilt to
face the sunrise on 15th August, the
actual day of the Feast of the
Assumption, creating a difference of
direction between chancel and nave.
Beckley has inspired writers,
including R.D. Blackmore (the author
of *Lorna Doone*), who set his novel
Cripps the Carrier (published in
1877) in the Beckley area. It is said
that Lewis Carroll had the idea of
Alice's chess-board in *Through the
Looking Glass* after looking down on
Otmoor from Beckley. That was
when the view from Beckley,
especially at sunset, was of little
fields covered by grass, rushes and
sedge of many different colours.

A thatched cottage at Beckley.

Follow this track from Woodperry.

Turn left off the road towards Woodperry.

OS. SP 41/51
& SP 40/ 50

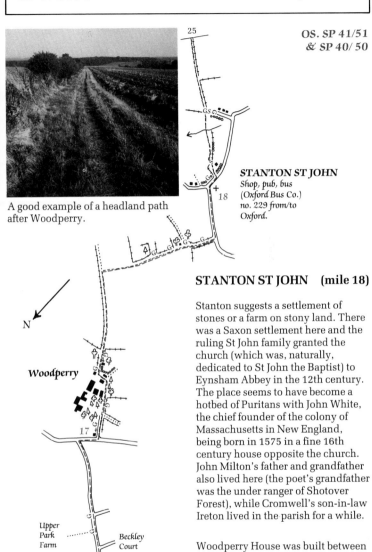

A good example of a headland path
after Woodperry.

STANTON ST JOHN
Shop, pub, bus
(Oxford Bus Co.)
no. 229 from/to
Oxford.

N

STANTON ST JOHN (mile 18)

Stanton suggests a settlement of
stones or a farm on stony land. There
was a Saxon settlement here and the
ruling St John family granted the
church (which was, naturally,
dedicated to St John the Baptist) to
Eynsham Abbey in the 12th century.
The place seems to have become a
hotbed of Puritans with John White,
the chief founder of the colony of
Massachusetts in New England,
being born in 1575 in a fine 16th
century house opposite the church.
John Milton's father and grandfather
also lived here (the poet's grandfather
was the under ranger of Shotover
Forest), while Cromwell's son-in-law
Ireton lived in the parish for a while.

Woodperry House was built between
1725 and 1731 for John Morse, a
London banker. Another banker,
John Thomson, bought it in 1879 and
the house remained in the Thomson
family's hands until 1976.

The tower of St John the Baptist church, Stanton St John.

OS. SP 40/50

FOREST HILL (mile 19)

Forest Hill is not named after a forest
but after the frosty nature of its ridge.
The church is largely Norman and is
where the poet Milton was married
to his first wife, Mary Powell.

FOREST HILL
*Pub, bus (Oxford
Bus Co.) nos. 2 & 280
from/to Oxford.
B&B at Manor Farm,
Forest Hill, Oxon.
T08677 2434
& with Mrs A Dunkley,
Mead Close, Forest
Hill, Oxon. T08677
2248.*

The
King's
Arms

Follow the line of the right of way
across this field to reach Forest Hill.

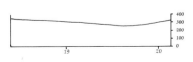

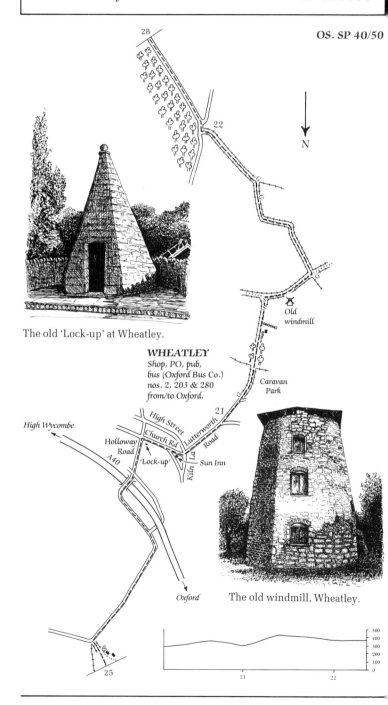

OS. SP 40/50

28

22

N

The old 'Lock-up' at Wheatley.

Old windmill

WHEATLEY
*Shop, PO, pub,
bus (Oxford Bus Co.)
nos. 2, 203 & 280
from/to Oxford.*

Caravan
Park

High Wycombe

High Street

21

Church Rd

Holloway
Road

A40

'Lock-up'

Kiln La.

Lutterworth Road

Sun Inn

Oxford

The old windmill, Wheatley.

25

The Sun Inn, Wheatley.

WHEATLEY   (mile 21)

Wheatley means a clearing where wheat grows. It was famous for its highwaymen and rowdy coaching inns in the 18th and early 19th century, however. Then, as now, it was on the main road between London and Oxford. The locals enjoyed pastimes such as cock-fighting and bull-baiting in a pit near the lock-up, which was built in 1834. In 'The Pattern of the Past' (1969), Guy Underwood reported that the sites of lock-ups (also known as 'blind houses' because of their lack of windows) all have a geodetic characteristic in common. Each is set in the centre of a 'reversed circle', which is a pattern produced when two water lines cross each other approximately at right angles to produce four C shaped spirals facing

outwards. This 'reversed circle' is also completely enclosed by a loop of one or more water lines. Places of execution share this characteristic. This pattern must, therefore, have been the reason for the placing of the lock-up, rather than the lock-up or its prisoners causing the pattern. Water lines are associated with the Mother Goddess, so the site's enclosure by water lines suggests that inmates were given to the Mother Goddess. The C shaped spirals facing outwards suggest a lack of divine protection, however. Your route through Wheatley also passes the Sun, an 18th century coaching inn, and a ruined mill which was built in the 18th century (on a medieval site) and was in use until 1915.

CUDDESDON (mile 23)

Cuddesdon means Cuthwine's Hill, but it is the Bishops of Oxford who have resided here since 1635. Their palace was burnt down in the Civil War and rebuilt in 1679. It was the obvious choice to site a theological college in 1853. The cruciform parish church is a magnificent example of Norman building work.

Ripon College, Cuddesdon.

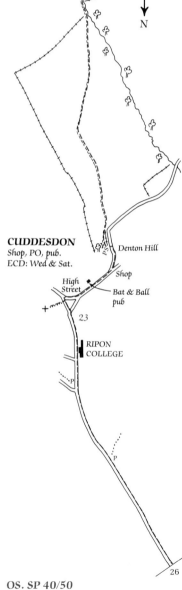

29

24

N

CUDDESDON
Shop, PO, pub.
ECD: Wed & Sat.

Denton Hill

Shop

High
Street

Bat & Ball
pub

+

23

RIPON
COLLEGE

P

P

26

500
400
300
200
100
0

23

24

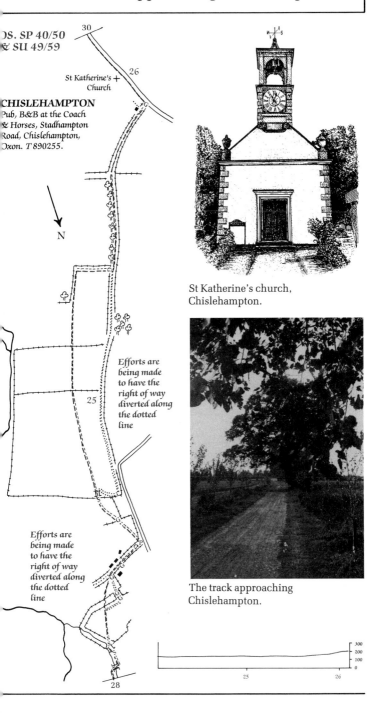

OS. SP 40/50
& SU 49/59

St Katherine's +
Church

CHISLEHAMPTON
Pub, B&B at the Coach
& Horses, Stadhampton
Road, Chislehampton,
Oxon. T 890255.

N

*Efforts are
being made
to have the
right of way
diverted along
the dotted
line*

*Efforts are
being made
to have the
right of way
diverted along
the dotted
line*

St Katherine's church,
Chislehampton.

The track approaching
Chislehampton.

OS. SU 49/59

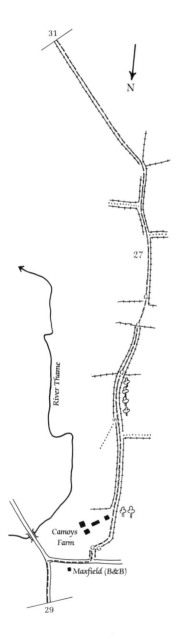

Turn left off the road at Camoys Farm, Chislehampton.

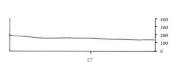

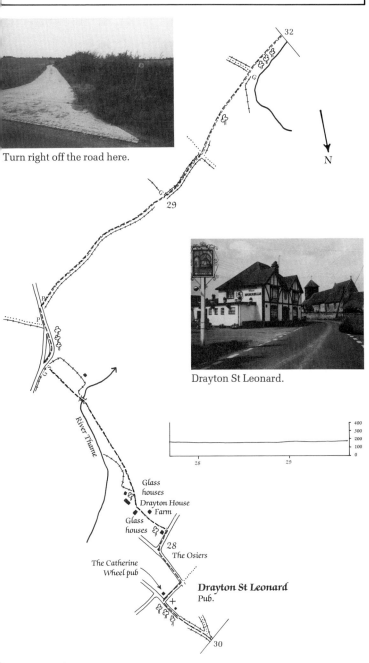

Turn right off the road here.

32

N

29

Drayton St Leonard.

River Thame

P

G

400
300
200
100
0

28   29

Glass
houses
Drayton House
Farm
Glass
houses

28
The Osiers

The Catherine
Wheel pub

Drayton St Leonard
Pub.

30

OS. SU 49/59

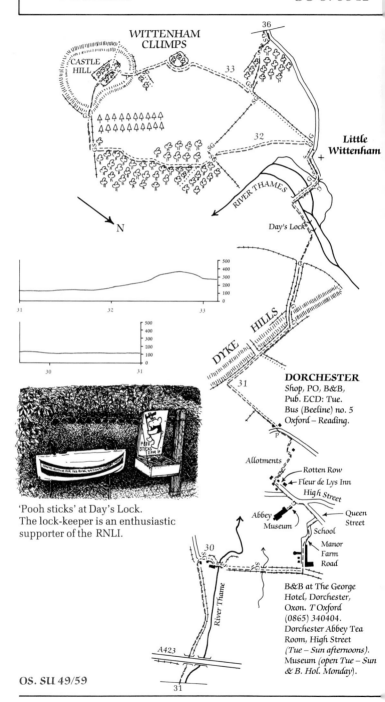

WITTENHAM
CLUMPS

CASTLE
HILL

36

33

32

Little
Wittenham

N

RIVER THAMES

Day's Lock

500
400
300
200
100
0

31   32   33

500
400
300
200
100
0

30   31

DYKE HILLS

31

DORCHESTER
Shop, PO, B&B,
Pub. ECD: Tue.
Bus (Beeline) no. 5
Oxford – Reading.

P

Allotments

Rotten Row
Fleur de Lys Inn
High Street
Queen
Street

Abbey
Museum

School

Manor
Farm
Road

'Pooh sticks' at Day's Lock.
The lock-keeper is an enthusiastic
supporter of the RNLI.

30

River Thame

A423

31

B&B at The George
Hotel, Dorchester,
Oxon. T Oxford
(0865) 340404.
Dorchester Abbey Tea
Room, High Street
(Tue – Sun afternoons).
Museum (open Tue – Sun
& B. Hol. Monday).

OS. SU 49/59

The George Hotel, Dorchester.

DORCHESTER   (mile 30)

Now just a village, Dorchester is in
reality one of England's oldest cities.
The earthworks of the Dyke Hills
between the River Thames at Day's
Lock and modern Dorchester mark
the site of an ancient British
stronghold which was protected by
the river on three sides and by the
massive banks and ditches on the
fourth side. A small Roman town
replaced this settlement, near the
river crossing on the Roman road
between Alchester and Silchester.
Excavations in 1962 showed that
timber-framed houses protected by
an earthen rampart were erected in
the allotment area by 200 AD. These
allotments are passed by the
Oxfordshire Trek, to the west of
Dorchester Abbey. By 400 a stone
wall had been built in front of the
earthen rampart and the town still
existed in the early 6th century,
when 'Dorocina' was occupied by
Saxons. The importance of this place
was emphasised in the early 7th

century. 38 years after St Augustine
came to Canterbury, St Berin
(Birinus) was consecrated bishop by
Pope Honorius I at Genoa in Italy and
landed in southern England in 634.
He converted King Cynegils of
Wessex, baptising him with many of
his subjects beside the River Thame
in Dorchester. Cynegils was an
ancestor of Alfred the Great, so this
was an important event. Oswald, the
Christian King of Northumbria, was
visiting Cynegils at the time, seeking
his daughter's hand in marriage, so
he stood as godfather. The two kings
gave Bishop Birinus 'the city of
Dorcic' as his See, so Dorchester
became the centre of Christianity in
Wessex. Birinus died in 649 and was
buried in Dorchester, but his remains
were later taken to Winchester,
which took over from Dorchester
when the Mercians threatened this
border area. The Mercians were to
make Dorchester their cathedral city
too, but the Normans transferred the

The track approaching Dorchester.

see to Lincoln and the cathedral at Dorchester became a collegiate college until the foundation of the Augustinian abbey of St Peter, St Paul and St Birinus in 1140, by Bishop Alexander of Lincoln. This was dissolved in 1536 and granted to Edmund Ashfield. Richard Beauforest saved the church from destruction by buying it for £140 and

giving it to the parish. The West tower was rebuilt in 1602.

The abbey's glory is its unique Jesse Tree in the north window of the chancel. This is a window showing the family tree of Jesus, starting at the bottom with Jesse, the father of King David. The figures of the Virgin and child and Christ at the top have been smashed, probably by Cromwell's soldiers. The 12th century font is also of interest, being made of lead. A ledge stone in the south nave aisle commemorates Sarah Fletcher, who died in 1799 'a martyr to excessive sensibility'. Her sea captain husband deserted her for another woman and she committed suicide (her ghost in her old cottage being recently exorcised). Another ledge stone commemorates the archdeacon of Dol, Brittany, who died here in 1798 after fleeing from the French Revolution.

Outside, near the porch, stands a 14th century church cross. The abbey guest house now houses a small museum, and has also served as a school. Across the road, on the route of this walk is the Fleur de Lys Inn, dating from about 1530. The really ancient sites are south, by the River Thames, however. The Thames is met at Day's Lock for the first, but not the last time on this walk. The Ordnance Survey/Nicholson Guide to the River Thames, edited by David Perrott, is the complete leisure guide for exploring this river. The Oxfordshire Trek crosses the foot-

Dorchester Abbey.

Day's Lock.

Looking back from the ramparts of Castle Hill.

bridge to Little Wittenham. On the way you will see 'Pooh sticks' for sale (proceeds to the Royal National Lifeboat Institution). You can toss these into the water on the upstream side of the bridge and marvel, like Winnie the Pooh, as they float under the bridge to be seen from the downstream side.

Your path soon climbs to one of the most beautiful spots in the Thames Valley – Wittenham Clumps. Castle Hill has ancient earthworks around its summit. A ditch on the eastern side, known as the Money Pit, was believed to contain buried treasure guarded by a phantom raven. The West Saxons of Wessex are known to have fought King Offa's Mercians here in the 8th century. This area was of immense significance in ancient times, however. The site of a Neolithic sacred complex between Dorchester and Clifton Hampden has been drowned by a lake in an old gravel pit, but it would have been near where Jon Michell's famous ley line, which runs across the country from St Michael's Mount in Cornwall via Glastonbury Tor and Avebury, would have crossed the Thames.

The gateway to Wittenham Clumps.

The view over the Thames valley towards Oxford from Castle Hill.

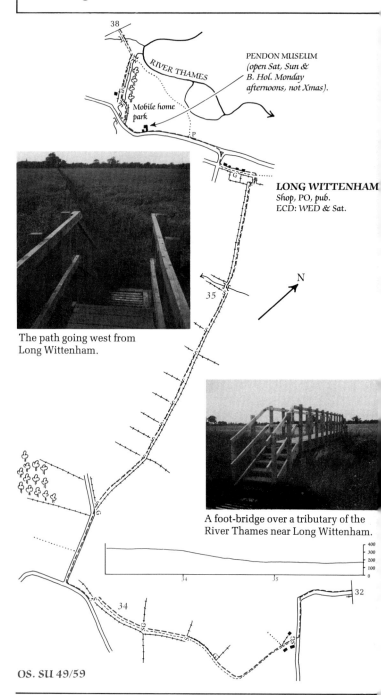

PENDON MUSEUM
*(open Sat, Sun &
B. Hol. Monday
afternoons, not Xmas).*

RIVER THAMES

Mobile home
park

P

LONG WITTENHAM
Shop, PO, pub.
ECD: *WED & Sat.*

N

The path going west from
Long Wittenham.

A foot-bridge over a tributary of the
River Thames near Long Wittenham.

OS. SU 49/59

Wittenham Clumps.

LONG WITTENHAM   (mile 36)

Try to arrange to walk through Long Wittenham on a Saturday or Sunday afternoon. You will be rewarded by the opportunity to visit a unique little museum, the Pendon Museum. In the early years of the 20th century, a little boy in Western Australia played with his tin-plate train set and fell in love with the railways of England. He vowed to ride them and make models of them for all to enjoy. At the age of 18, in 1925, he came to live with relatives at Wanborough, in the Vale of the White Horse, near the railway town of Swindon. He found himself in the paradise of his childhood but he also realised that changes were afoot. A gem of a 15th century building in Wanborough itself was mutilated with a suburban type front soon after his arrival. Even the Great Western Railway was

experimenting with diesel locomotion. He teamed up with two other enthusiasts from Bristol to make a faithful model of a village which they called Pendon Parva, representing the peaceful villages of the Vale of the White Horse in the 1930s, with detailed models of the thatched cottages, the farms, the fields and the quiet country lanes. The Australian, Roye England, appreciated what locals took for granted and allowed to be destroyed. He bought an old public house in Long Wittenham and converted it into a youth hostel. The hostellers saw his models and spread the news far and wide. The railways and the countryside of the 1930s have been preserved in miniature in what is now the Pendon Museum.

OS. SU 49/59

41

Didcot Power Station ←

→ N

37

British Rail station

Didcot ←

Appleford Train

Chambrai Close

→ Oxford

School Lane

THAMES

36

36

APPLEFORD (mile 37)

John Faulkner, who lived to be the world's oldest jockey, lies buried in the church of St Peter and Paul. He rode his first winner aged eight and rode his last race at Abingdon races when 74. He died in 1933 at the age of 104.

Didcot Power Station.

Appleford station.

The view from the foot-bridge over Culham Cut.

All Saint's church, Sutton Courtenay.

Sutton Pools.

SUTTON COURTENAY (mile 39)

Sutton Courtenay was given to Abingdon Abbey in 687, but the 'abbey' built here in 1350 was probably just for use as the abbot's summer residence. It is now used for conferences, including the Gandhi Foundation's annual summer school. The Dalai Lama has been received here. The parish church is also of interest as its churchyard contains two tombs of famous people. Herbert Henry Asquith, Earl of Oxford and Asquith, was the last Liberal Prime Minister (from 1908 to 1916). He was buried here in 1928 after living in the village for some years. Eric Blair is also buried here. His pen-name was George Orwell (of *Animal Farm* and *1984* fame) and several of the yew trees beside the churchyard path were planted in his memory.

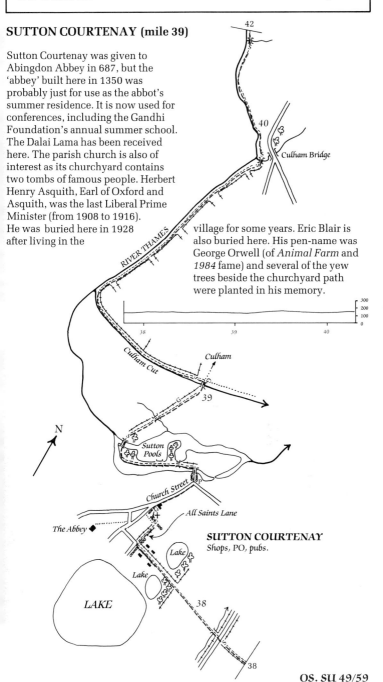

SUTTON COURTENAY
Shops, PO, pubs.

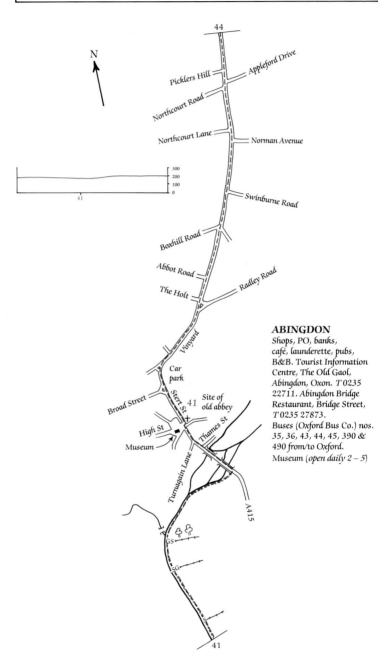

ABINGDON
*Shops, PO, banks,
café, launderette, pubs,
B&B. Tourist Information
Centre, The Old Gaol,
Abingdon, Oxon. T 0235
22711. Abingdon Bridge
Restaurant, Bridge Street,
T 0235 27873.
Buses (Oxford Bus Co.) nos.
35, 36, 43, 44, 45, 390 &
490 from/to Oxford.
Museum (open daily 2 – 5)*

Looking back from the bridge over the River Thames at Abingdon.

ABINGDON   (mile 41)

Abingdon is the biggest town on this walk, and is reached just when its facilities would probably be most needed. An ancient market town, it derives its name from being on the site of an even older abbey (dating from at least the 7th century).The Tourist Information Centre is located in the Old Gaol, built in 1810 and now an Arts and Sports Centre. The Benedictine abbey of St Mary was probably founded in 675 in Bagley Wood, near Sunningwell, but soon moved to Abingdon. It was dissolved in 1538. There were traditionally twin foundations for men and women by Hean and his sister Cilla, but only the former prospered. The abbey was refounded in 954 under St Ethelwold, a pupil of St Dunstan, by King Edred after it had been sacked by Danes. Everything but the gatehouse and a few minor buildings by the millstream disappeared at the Dissolution. The outlines of the church and cloisters were excavated in 1922 in Abbey House gardens. A line of checker (exchequer) buildings can still be visited, while the abbey gate stands beside St Nicholas's church. Relics of the abbey are on display in the Abingdon Museum,

which is housed in the Old County Hall, built in 1677, possibly to designs by Sir Christopher Wren, when Abingdon was the county town of Berkshire. There is also a display of buns which are traditionally thrown from the roof of the Old County Hall to the assembled crowd below on special occasions – such as visits by royalty.

Cross this stile out of Abingdon.

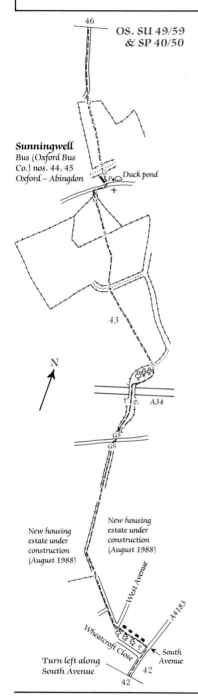

OS. SU 49/59
& SP 40/50

Sunningwell
Bus (Oxford Bus
Co.) nos. 44, 45
Oxford – Abingdon

Duck pond

N

43

New housing
estate under
construction
(August 1988)

New housing
estate under
construction
(August 1988)

West Avenue

A34

A4183

Wheatcroft Close

South
Avenue

Turn left along
South Avenue

42

42

SUNNINGWELL (mile 43)

St Leonard's church is well worth a
visit. Its tower was used by Roger
Bacon for his experiments with
telescopes in the 13th century. It is
the church's remarkable seven-sided
porch which catches the eye,
however. This was a present from
Bishop Jewel of Salisbury, who was
rector of Sunningwell in 1551. Jewel
was a Protestant who fled to Germany
in 1555 when Mary acceded to the
throne. He returned with the
accession of Elizabeth I to be
consecrated Bishop of Salisbury. He
died in 1571. Another famous
incumbent was Dr Samuel Fell, who
became Dean of Christ Church
College, Oxford. A fervent Royalist,
he died of a broken heart at the news
of Charles I's execution. Before that
he had been evicted from the
university for being a Royalist. When
the Chancellor of Oxford, the Earl of
Pembroke, came to evict him, he told
Pembroke that 'he was too
inconsiderable a person to parley
with'. The outraged earl sent Fell to
prison and turned his family out of
the Deanery. The outspoken Dr Fell
had himself threatened to send down
an undergraduate from Christ
Church. He gave the student one
chance, however, to immediately
translate from the Latin Martial's
epigram on Sabidius, the literal
translation of which is 'I do not love
thee, Sabidius, nor can I say why. I
can only say this, I do not love thee'.
The student translated:
'I do not love thee, Dr Fell,
    The reason why, I cannot tell;
    But this I know, and know full
well,
    I do not love thee, Dr Fell.'

The unique seven-sided porch of St Leonard's church, Sunningwell.

OS. SP 40/50

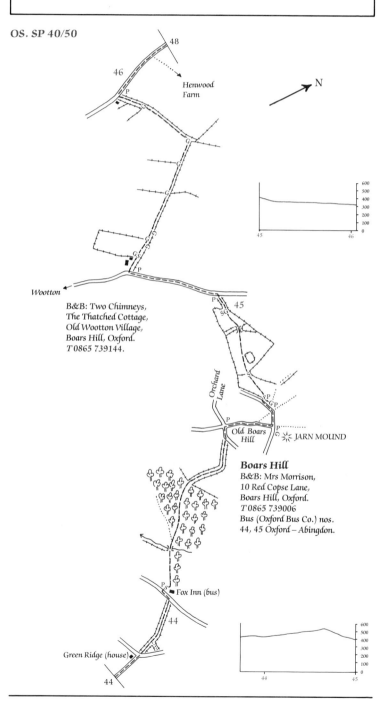

48

46

Henwood
Farm

N

Wootton

B&B: Two Chimneys,
The Thatched Cottage,
Old Wootton Village,
Boars Hill, Oxford.
T 0865 739144.

45

Orchard
Lane

Old Boars
Hill

JARN MOUND

Boars Hill
B&B: Mrs Morrison,
10 Red Copse Lane,
Boars Hill, Oxford.
T 0865 739006
Bus (Oxford Bus Co.) nos.
44, 45 Oxford – Abingdon.

Fox Inn (bus)

44

Green Ridge (house)

44

The path from the Fox Inn.

Matthew Arnold's Field. Bear left along the private road (but public footpath) to a stile in the fence on your right. DO NOT go ahead through the gate beside this notice.

BOAR'S HILL (mile 44)

Jarn Mound viewpoint and wild garden were created by Sir Arthur Evans 'who loved antiquity, nature, freedom and youth' for 'all to enjoy'. He gave work to unemployed Welsh miners during the Depression. The view over the tops of the trees can include the White Horse of Uffington, Red Horse Hill in Warwickshire, Inkpen Beacon, Wychwood Forest and the Chilterns, so come on a clear day if you can. This area is also linked with the Victorian poet Matthew Arnold, who wrote *The Scholar Gipsy* and *Thyrsis*.

BESSELS LEIGH   (mile 47)

Bessels Leigh took its name from the family which provided the stone to build Abingdon bridge in 1416. The Manor House was later bought by William Lenthall, who was MP for Woodstock. He was the Speaker of the Long Parliament. When Charles I attempted to arrest five MPs in January 1640, he said:
'May it please your majesty, I have neither eyes to see nor tongue to speak in this place, but as the House is pleased to direct me, whose servant I am here, and humbly beg your majesty's pardon that I cannot give any other answer'. The Manor House was ruined in the Civil War.

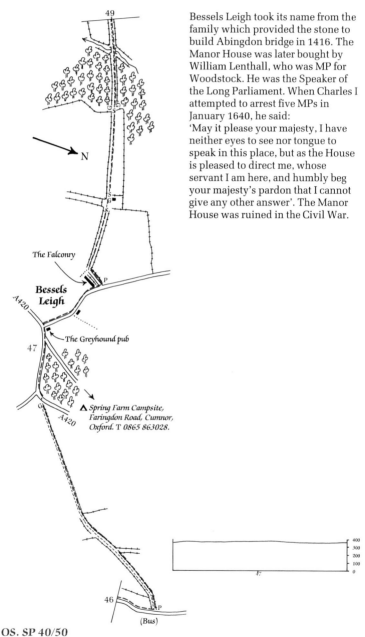

The Falconry

Bessels Leigh

A420

The Greyhound pub

47

A420

⌂ Spring Farm Campsite, Faringdon Road, Cumnor, Oxford. T 0865 863028.

400
300
200
100
0

46

(Bus)

OS. SP 40/50

OS. SP 40/50

APPLETON   (mile 48)

The Manor House at Appleton has survived and contains Norman and Tudor work. It is situated near St Laurence's church, which is basically Norman with a 15th century tower.

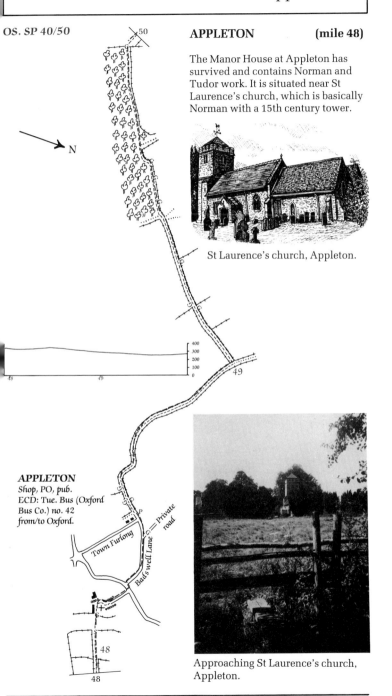

St Laurence's church, Appleton.

APPLETON
*Shop, PO, pub.
ECD: Tue. Bus (Oxford
Bus Co.) no. 42
from/to Oxford.*

Town Furlong

Bad's well Lane

Private road

Approaching St Laurence's church, Appleton.

OS. SP 40/50

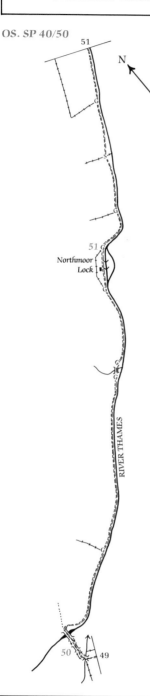

A boat leaving Northmoor Lock.

Cross the River Thames by this foot-bridge one mile south of Northmoor Lock.

OS. SP 40/50

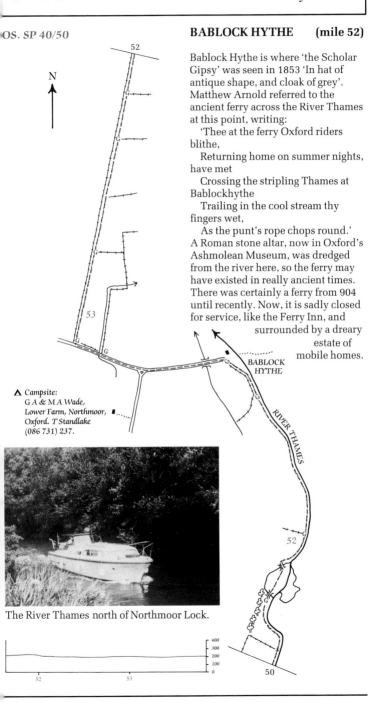

BABLOCK HYTHE   (mile 52)

Bablock Hythe is where 'the Scholar Gipsy' was seen in 1853 'In hat of antique shape, and cloak of grey'. Matthew Arnold referred to the ancient ferry across the River Thames at this point, writing:

'Thee at the ferry Oxford riders blithe,

Returning home on summer nights, have met

Crossing the stripling Thames at Bablockhythe

Trailing in the cool stream thy fingers wet,

As the punt's rope chops round.'

A Roman stone altar, now in Oxford's Ashmolean Museum, was dredged from the river here, so the ferry may have existed in really ancient times. There was certainly a ferry from 904 until recently. Now, it is sadly closed for service, like the Ferry Inn, and surrounded by a dreary estate of mobile homes.

BABLOCK HYTHE

RIVER THAMES

△ Campsite:
G A & M A Wade,
Lower Farm, Northmoor,
Oxford. T Standlake
(086 731) 237.

The River Thames north of Northmoor Lock.

OS. SP 40/50

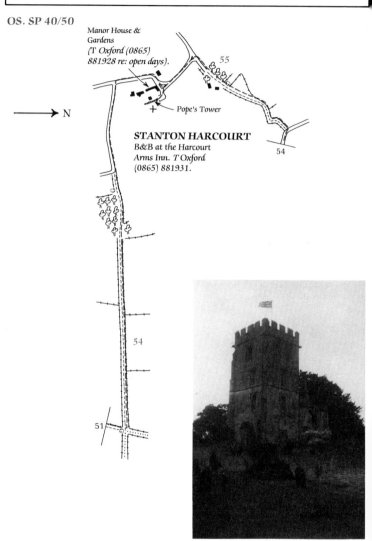

Manor House &
Gardens
(T Oxford (0865)
881928 re: open days).

55

Pope's Tower

→ N

STANTON HARCOURT
*B&B at the Harcourt
Arms Inn. T Oxford
(0865) 881931.*

54

54

51

Pope's Tower, Stanton Harcourt.

STANTON HARCOURT   (mile 55)

An ancient stone circle was erected near here about 2500 BC. These stones gave their name to the village (Stanton meaning settlement of stones). It was said that the devil curses anyone disturbing the stones and it is a fact that when an airfield was laid out on the ancient site in 1940 the men constructing the airfield were strafed by a German fighting plane. Some of the stones still exist scattered about and their original holes were uncovered in the 1970s, when a ditch was found to have encircled them. It was planned in August 1988 to re-erect the remaining stones and to replace the missing ones with concrete replicas. The original stones are made out of naturally concreted gravel. The second half of the village's name comes from the Harcourt family who used to reside here. The Harcourt family ancestry has been traced back to Bernard the Dane, second in command to Rollo (later Duke of Normandy) on his invasion of France in 876. The beautiful and harmoniously designed church is dedicated to St Michael, which is significant given the presence of the stone circle and the link between St Michael and ley, or earth energy, lines.

The church was built in 1130 by Queen Adeliza, the second wife of Henry I, who then owned the manor of Stanton. Its chancel is divided from the nave by what is said to be the oldest surviving wooden screen in England. The figure of St Etheldreda or Audrey, the 7th century abbess of Ely (from whom we get the word 'tawdry' - she liked cheap jewellery as a child), is painted on it. Note too the tomb of Sir Robert Harcourt on the north wall. He was standard bearer to Henry VII at the Battle of Bosworth in 1485 and the remains of the actual standard hang above his tomb.

On the outside wall of the south transept, is a medieval 'mass dial' dated 1359. This was a sun dial to determine the time for mass to be said. Above it is a memorial plaque to John Hewet and Sarah Drew with an epitaph by the poet Alexander Pope. While staying in 'Pope's Tower' in 1718, he wrote to his friend Lady Mary Montegu about an accident in a field here - two lovers, about to be wed, were killed by lightning on 31st July, 1718. They were buried together in the churchyard. John Hewet was 25 and Sarah Drew was 18.

'Think not by rigorous judgement seiz'd,
    A pair so faithful could expire,
    Victims so pure heav'n saw well pleased
    And snatched them in celestial fire.

Live well and fear no sudden fate,
When God calls virtue to the grave,
Alike its justice soon or late,
Mercy alike to kill or save.

Virtue unmov'd can hear the call
And face the flash that melts the ball.'

Alexander Pope finished his translation of the 'Iliad' in the tower that is named after him. It is actually the 15th century gatehouse to the Manor House, which contains a fine, intact, medieval kitchen. It is possible to visit the Manor House and Gardens on certain days (Oxford 881928 for details).

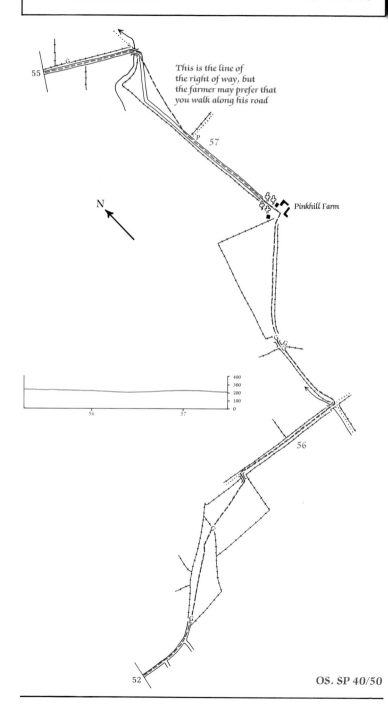

This is the line of
the right of way, but
the farmer may prefer that
you walk along his road

Pinkhill Farm

N

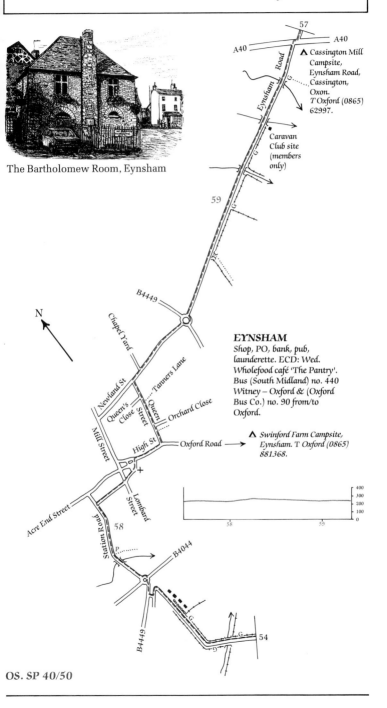

The Bartholomew Room, Eynsham

A40   57

A40

▲ Cassington Mill
Campsite,
Eynsham Road,
Cassington,
Oxon.
T Oxford (0865)
62997.

Eynsham Road

Caravan
Club site
(members
only)

59

B4449

N

Chapel Yard

Newland St

Queen's Close

Tanners Lane

Queen Street

Orchard Close

Mill Street

High St

Oxford Road →

Acre End Street

Lombard Street

Station Road

58

P

B4044

B4449

54

EYNSHAM

*Shop, PO, bank, pub,
launderette. ECD: Wed.
Wholefood café 'The Pantry'.
Bus (South Midland) no. 440
Witney – Oxford & (Oxford
Bus Co.) no. 90 from/to
Oxford.*

▲ *Swinford Farm Campsite,
Eynsham. T Oxford (0865)
881368.*

400
300
200
100
0

58   59

OS. SP 40/50

The Red Lion, Eynsham.

EYNSHAM

(mile 58)

An important Benedictine abbey was founded here in 1005. Aelfric, the Anglo-Saxon scholar and grammarian, was its first abbot and Eynsham's importance in Saxon days is indicated by the fact that Ethelred the Unready once summoned his Witan (Saxon parliament) here. The Benedictine abbey was dispersed at the Norman Conquest but refounded by 1086 by Bishop Remigius of Lincoln and moved to Stow in 1091. It was re-established about 1109, however, and stayed put until it was dissolved and given to the Earl of Derby in 1539. Nothing remains of the abbey, but the cross in the square opposite St Leonard's church may equal it in age. It used to be 20 feet high. St Leonard is the patron saint of prisoners and opposite the church, near the remains of the cross, is the Bartholomew Room. This was built as a school with money left by John Bartholomew when he died in 1724. His will also provided for the education of ten poor boys from Eynsham. The building later served as a prison, however.

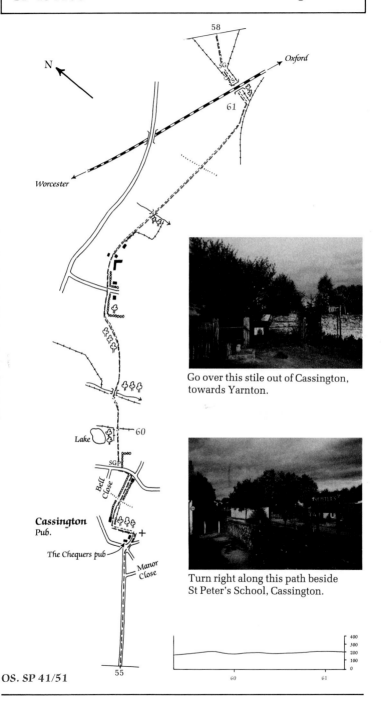

58

Oxford

N

61

Worcester

Cassington
Pub.

Lake — 60

Bell Close

SG

Cassington
Pub.

The Chequers pub

Manor Close

Go over this stile out of Cassington,
towards Yarnton.

Turn right along this path beside
St Peter's School, Cassington.

55

OS. SP 41/51

59

YARNTON (mile 61)

The church here is worth visiting. It has an interesting medieval reredos given by William Fletcher, Alderman of Oxford, who lies under a table top, decorated with a small brass. There is a fine 13th century Cross in the churchyard and a Jacobean manor house nearby.

N

Frogwelldown La

62

YARNTON
Pub, bus (South Midland) nos.420, 421, 423 Oxford – Woodstock.

57

Pound Close

Red Lion pub

Go over this stile towards Yarnton.

62

OS. SP 41/51

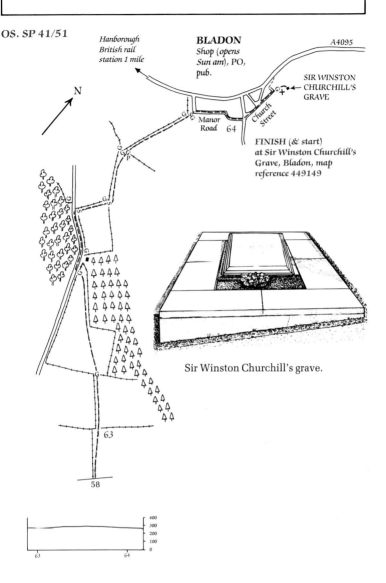

Hanborough
British rail
station 1 mile

BLADON
Shop (*opens
Sun am*), PO,
pub.

A4095

SIR WINSTON
CHURCHILL'S
GRAVE

N

Church Street

G

Manor
Road   64

FINISH (& start)
at Sir Winston Churchill's
Grave, Bladon, map
reference 449149

63

58

Sir Winston Churchill's grave.

400
300
200
100
0

63   64

Transport and accommodation

Public transport comes into its own on the Oxfordshire Trek. By far the best plan is to walk the route in sections from bus stop or railway station to another bus stop or railway station, with Oxford as your base. Convenient sections could be:
Bladon – Islip (11 miles, or 12 miles from Hanborough railway station to Gosford bus stop); Islip – Wheatley (10 miles, or 12 miles from Gosford bus stop); Wheatley – Dorchester (9 miles); Dorchester – Abingdon (11 miles); Abingdon – Eynsham (17 miles); Eynsham – Bladon (6 miles, with time to visit Blenheim Palace and bus back to Oxford from Woodstock). Try to avoid Dorchester on a Monday (the day the museum is closed) and try to pass Long Wittenham (between Dorchester and Abingdon) on a weekend afternoon (when Pendon Museum is open). Information on train services is available from British Rail (Oxford 722333), while information on bus services is available from the Oxford Bus Co (Oxford 711312), South Midland (Witney 776679) and from Beeline (Reading 581358).

There is a full range of accommodation along this route. In addition to those listed, addresses are available from the Tourist Information Centre, St Aldate's, Oxford, OX1 1DY (Oxford 726871). Oxford Youth Hostel is in Jack Straw's Lane, Headington, Oxford (Oxford 62997). Membership details from the YHA, Trevelyan House, 8 St Stephen's Hill, St Alban's, Herts, AL1 2DY. Two campsites near the centre of Oxford are Oxford Camping International, 426 Abingdon Road, Oxford, OX1 4XN (Oxford 246551) and Salter Bros Ltd, Slipway, Meadow Lane, Donnington Bridge Road, Oxford (Oxford 723534). There is also a campsite at Templars Court Country Club, Sandford-on-Thames, Oxford (Oxford 779359). Always check bus and train timetables in advance as these services are liable to alteration. Oxford is a magnet for tourists so, if possible, book accommodation well in advance. If you base yourself in Oxford for a week, you should have time to complete this walk and to visit the city and university, some of whose attractions are Christ Church College, Cathedral and Meadow, the view from the tower of St Mary's Church in the High, the Bodleian Library, the Sheldonian Theatre, 'The Oxford Story', the Ashmolean Museum, the University Museum, Pitt Rivers Museum, Magdalen College, the Botanic Garden and the Museum of Oxford. You can hire a punt at Folly Bridge, Magdalen Bridge or the Cherwell Boathouse, or take a Salters Boat trip between Folly Bridge, Oxford and Abingdon Bridge, which is on the Oxfordshire Trek. South Midland run open top bus tours from Oxford to Blenheim Palace and Woodstock.

A British Rail Sprinter train roars over the tunnel by which the footpath approaches Yarnton. This train runs between Oxford and Worcester and calls at Hanborough station, just one mile west of the start and finish of The Oxfordshire Trek at Bladon.

Diamond Farm Campsite, Bletchingdon.

Index

The swan population on the River Thames is, thankfully, on the increase since the banning on the 1st January 1987 of the use of lead weights by anglers. There are now about 808 swans and 220 cygnets on the river, up from 675 swans and 152 cygnets in 1983. The swans ingested discarded or lost weights while grubbing for food on the river bed, and were subsequently poisoned. There is evidence, however, that *some* anglers are disregarding the law, and are still using lead weights, since 20% of recently recorded swan deaths were found to be due to lead poisoning.

64 Key to strip maps

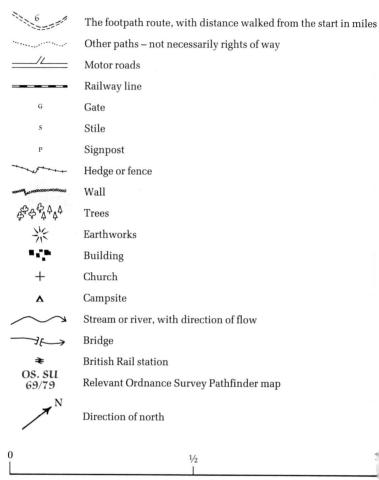

The footpath route, with distance walked from the start in miles

Other paths – not necessarily rights of way

Motor roads

Railway line

G   Gate

S   Stile

P   Signpost

Hedge or fence

Wall

Trees

Earthworks

Building

Church

Campsite

Stream or river, with direction of flow

Bridge

British Rail station

OS. SU
69/79   Relevant Ordnance Survey Pathfinder map

N

Direction of north

0   ½

Scale in miles

Each map has a profile of the walk showing the height in feet above sea level and the distance in miles from the start.

Laurence Main is a voluntary footpaths secretary for the Ramblers' Association.
If you are interested in joining the Ramblers' Association, please write for full details to: The Ramblers' Association, 1/5 Wandsworth Road, London SW8 2XX, enclosing a large sae.